A
SCRIPTURAL OUTLINE
OF THE
BAPTISM
IN THE
HOLY SPIRIT

A SCRIPTURAL OUTLINE

OF THE

BAPTISM

IN THE

HOLY SPIRIT

GEORGE & HARRIET GILLIES

📖 *Whitaker House*

A SCRIPTURAL OUTLINE OF THE BAPTISM IN THE HOLY SPIRIT

ISBN: 0-88368-062-9
Printed in the United States of America
Copyright © 1972, 1998 by Whitaker House

Whitaker House
30 Hunt Valley Circle
New Kensington, PA 15068

13 14 15 16 17 18 19 20 21 / 05 04 03 02 01 00 99 98

Contents

Foreword

It was midnight. I was waiting in the lobby of the Mission Inn at Riverside, California, where I had just witnessed how the Lord Jesus baptized a Colorado lawyer in the Holy Spirit. We were going for a cup of coffee before we would turn to rest. In walked two friends, and I was introduced to George and Harriet Gillies. Quickly the lawyer told him his experience, which, unrealized by George, Harriet had received all by herself some six months before. George was thrilled and anxious to get the same blessing. We agreed to meet sometime the next day, but that meeting never came off.

George and Harriet decided to listen to my tapes if they could not speak to me. They began to examine this teaching and made a deep study of the Scriptures. The result was that George also received the baptism in the Holy Spirit in his private devotions, all alone with Jesus, who is the only Baptizer in the Holy Spirit.

George went about a very thorough and systematic method of research, just as he used to do in thirty-five years of business life. You will find the results in the following pages.

Not only in their personal lives, but also in the lives of scores of others, George and Harriet have been able to see the truth of these Scriptures. Over the past few years, their home has been a veritable "Bethel" to many weary seekers after Truth and reality. I have enjoyed repeated visits to their home and was able to witness how the Lord had built up their faith and used them to establish faith in others by the Scriptures.

I have ready almost all that has been published on the Holy Spirit, and I have been privileged to teach many others, yet I do not know anything quite as simple and still as effective as these studies as outlined by my friends. Much of it has been my personal approach to the matter for years. I recommend this booklet to all honest seekers after Truth, and would remind them that ultimately Jesus Christ is the Way, the Truth, and the Life.

These studies will confront you with Him and not with a doctrine. Your personal baptism will come through an encounter with your Lord and Savior. He is the Lamb of God (John 1:36) who took away your sin, and He is the Son of God who baptizes in the Holy Spirit (v. 33).

— DAVID J. DU PLESSIS

1

Who and What Is the Holy Spirit?

The Spirit of God — 1 Thessalonians 4:8.

The Spirit of Jesus Christ, the Son of God — John 14:18; Galatians 4:6.

The mind of Christ — Philippians 2:5.

The Spirit of truth — John 14:17; 15:26.

The Comforter — John 14:16, 26; 15:26; 16:7.

The Spirit of the Father — Matthew 10:20.

Power from on high — Luke 24:49.

A gift of God, just as salvation is — Acts 2:38; 8:20; Romans 5:5; 1 Thessalonians 4:8; Luke 11:13; Acts 11:17; 15:8; Galatians 3:2.

The promise of the Father — Luke 24:49; Acts 1:4; Galatians 3:14.

Power — Mark 9:1; Acts 1:8.

2

Where Is the Holy Spirit and When Does He Appear?

Here, always — Matthew 28:20; John 14:16; Luke 11:13.

He was with certain people prior to Pentecost, but not in them — John 7:39; 14:17–18.

Made available to all believers at Pentecost — Acts 2:38.

Now — Joel 2:28–29; Psalm 90:4; 2 Peter 3:8; Hebrews 13:8; Acts 2:39; Luke 11:13.

Available now to Gentiles — Ephesians 3:6.

3

Why Be Saved and Baptized in the Holy Spirit?

To become alive — John 6:63; Romans 8:11.

To become a child of God — John 1:12–13; Romans 8:14–21; Galatians 3:7–9, 14, 29; 4:6–7; 1 John 3:1–2.

To be of Christ — Romans 8:9; Galatians 2:20; 3:27.

To have life and peace — Romans 8:6; Galatians 2:20; 6:8.

To have no condemnation — Romans 8:1.

To be free from the law of sin and death — Romans 8:2–6, 9–10, 13; Galatians 2:19; 5:16–18.

So that *"the righteous requirement of the law might be fulfilled in us"* — Romans 8:4.

To be taught all things and to understand what Jesus said — John 6:63; 14:26; 1 Thessalonians 1:5; 1 John 2:20, 27.

To have the testimony of Jesus — John 15:26.

To be effective witnesses unto Jesus — Acts 1:8; John 20:21.

To be able to worship the Father in spirit and in truth — John 4:23–24.

To have Jesus glorified — John 16:14; Romans 8:18.

To receive the Promise of the Father — Luke 24:49; Acts 1:4; Galatians 3:14.

To know the joy that Jesus promised — John 3:29; 15:11; 16:20–24.

To follow Christ's example — Matthew 3:16; Mark 1:10; Luke 3:21–22; John 1:32.

To have a full and effective ministry — Luke 4:18–19; Isaiah 61:1–3.

To boldly proclaim the Gospel — Ephesians 6:18–20.

To receive the kingdom of God with power — Mark 9:1; Romans 14:17; Galatians 2:20.

To receive power from on high — Acts 1:8.

To be able not only to see, but also to enter into the kingdom of God — John 3:3–5.

To be partakers of the divine nature — 2 Peter 1:4; Romans 8:38–39; Exodus 9:16.

To be shown things to come, things of Jesus, and things of the Father — John 16:13–15.

To have the perfect prayer made when we do not know what to pray for — Romans 8:26.

To have intercession made for us — Romans 8:26–27.

The redemption of our bodies — Romans 8:23.

To help our weaknesses — Romans 8:26.

To follow the leading of the Spirit — Romans 8:5; Galatians 5:25.

To be guided into all truth — John 16:13; 1 John 2:20, 27.

To have righteousness, peace, and joy in the Spirit — Romans 14:17.

To be called according to God's purpose — Romans 8:28.

To have the Spirit *"of power and of love and of a sound mind"* — 2 Timothy 1:7.

To know that we are really baptized into one body, which is Christ's church — Ezekiel 36:26–27; 1 Corinthians 12:13; Galatians 3:26–29; Ephesians 1:13.

To have the fruit of the Spirit — Galatians 5:22–23; Ephesians 5:9.

4

Who Can Receive the Baptism in the Holy Spirit?

One who is a born-again believer — John 3:34; Matthew 18:3; Acts 2:38–39; 8:12–17.

One who is completely surrendered to God, obeying the Great Commandment — Matthew 22:35–38.

One who is a child of God — John 1:12.

One who receives the kingdom of God as a child — Mark 10:15.

One who is willing to become a fool for Christ — 1 Corinthians 3:18.

Anyone who meets the above conditions, whether he is a Jew or a Gentile — Ephesians 3:6.

5

Who Is the Baptizer in the Holy Spirit?

Jesus is the Baptizer — Matthew 3:11; Mark 1:7–8; Luke 3:16; John 1:33.

Jesus has the power to baptize in the Holy Spirit — Matthew 28:18.

6

How Do You Know for Sure That You Have Received the Baptism in the Holy Spirit?

The Spirit can dwell with people and yet not be in them — John 14:17.

After conversion, one is not necessarily baptized in the Holy Spirit. See the example in Samaria — Acts 8:14–16.

How did Peter and John know that the people had not received the baptism in the Holy Spirit? — Acts 8:16.

And then, how did Peter, John, and Simon the sorcerer know that the people had received the baptism after Peter and John had laid hands on them? — Acts 8:17.

Another example is the baptism at the house of Cornelius, a Gentile — Acts 10:1–48.

The Jews who went to the house of Cornelius with Peter were astonished, *"because the gift of the Holy Spirit had been poured out on the Gentiles also"* — Acts 10:45.

How did the Jews know that the Gentiles had received the baptism? *"For they heard them speak with tongues and magnify God"* — Acts 10:46.

The apostolic Jews in Jerusalem were very much upset, and so they contended with Peter for having gone to the Gentiles. They also could not believe that the Gentiles had been baptized in the Holy Spirit — Acts 11:1–3.

Peter told them, *"As I began to speak, the Holy Spirit fell upon them, as upon us at the beginning"* — Acts 11:15.

The beginning was at Pentecost, when *"they were all filled with the Holy Spirit and began to speak with other tongues, as the Spirit gave them utterance"* — Acts 2:4.

Then, *"When they heard these things they became silent; and they glorified God, saying, 'Then God has also granted to the Gentiles repentance to life'"* — Acts 11:18.

The baptism at Ephesus at the hands of Paul — Acts 19:1–6.

The evidence was praying in an unknown tongue — Acts 2:4; 10:46, 19:6; Mark 16:17; John 3:8; 1 Corinthians 14:22.

Jesus said everyone born of the Spirit would hear the sound thereof — John 3:8.

You are no holier after receiving the baptism than you were before. But you now potentially have the power of Jesus within you to overcome evil and to be a witness for Christ. The Lord God lets it be your choice, your free will, as to how you use this wonderful gift of God, or whether you bury this talent in the earth — Matthew 25:14–30; Acts 1:8.

7

What Are the Manifestations of the Holy Spirit?

The manifestations of the Holy Spirit are *"given to each one for the profit of all"* — 1 Corinthians 12:7.

1. The word of wisdom — 1 Corinthians 12:8.
2. The word of knowledge — 1 Corinthians 12:8.
3. Faith — 1 Corinthians 12:9.
4. Gifts of healing — 1 Corinthians 12:9.
5. The working of miracles — 1 Corinthians 12:10.
6. Prophecy — 1 Corinthians 12:10.
7. Discerning of Spirits — 1 Corinthians 12:10.
8. Different kinds of tongues — 1 Corinthians 12:10.

9. Interpretation of tongues — 1 Corinthians 12:10.

These manifestations of the Holy Spirit should be administered in the *"more excellent way"* (1 Corinthians 12:31), which is with love — 1 Corinthians 13:1–3; 14:1.

When you receive the baptism in the Holy Spirit, you get the potential to exercise all of the above nine manifestations. They are all in you. But you only use them one at a time as the Spirit leads you to do, for the Spirit divides all nine *"to each one individually as He wills"* — 1 Corinthians 12:11.

8

Manifestation of Prophecy Desired in the Church

You should desire to prophesy — 1 Corinthians 14:1, 39.

The purpose of prophecy is for *"edification and exhortation and comfort"* — 1 Corinthians 14:3.

Prophecy edifies the church — 1 Corinthians 14:4, 31.

Prophecy is greater in the church than even tongues (unless the tongues are interpreted) — 1 Corinthians 14:5.

Prophesying is for the believer — 1 Corinthians 14:22.

9

Manifestation of Tongues Is Highly Desired in Private Prayer, but Should Be Limited in Church

Paul was careful to separate the usage of tongues in the church from their use in private prayer — 1 Corinthians 14.

Jesus said that believers will speak in new tongues — Mark 16:17.

When you pray in a tongue that is unknown to you, you pray directly to God in the Spirit — 1 Corinthians 14:2.

You pray to God in spiritual "mysteries" — 1 Corinthians 14:2.

You worship God in spirit and in truth, as Jesus commanded — John 4:23–24; Psalm 51:15.

You edify yourself spiritually — 1 Corinthians 14:4; Ephesians 3:16; Romans 8:16; Jude 20.

You thank God with an absolute, unselfish prayer, a perfect prayer — 1 Corinthians 14:17.

You can know the meaning of *"Pray without ceasing"* — 1 Thessalonians 5:17.

When you do not know what to pray for, or are not sure how God wants you to pray about a situation, then pray in the Spirit, and you cannot miss — Romans 8:26.

The Spirit will pray for your infirmities (and those of others) for you *"with groanings which cannot be uttered"* by you — Romans 8:26–27.

It is desirable that all believers speak in tongues — 1 Corinthians 14:5, 37.

Always pray in the Spirit, so that you are able to boldly proclaim the Gospel — Ephesians 6:18–20; Acts 1:8.

The Lord commands that we do not forbid fellow believers to speak in tongues — 1 Corinthians 14:39.

Praying in tongues is a glory, *"I thank my God I speak with tongues more than you all"* — 1 Corinthians 14:18.

Singing with the Spirit is also a glory and a joy — 1 Corinthians 14:15.

Remember the power of what you speak. *"Death and life are in the power of the tongue"* — Proverbs 18:21.

10

Manifestation of Tongues in the Church

All manifestations of the Spirit are to *"be done decently and in order"* — 1 Corinthians 14:40.

In the church, praying in tongues should always be followed by interpretation — 1 Corinthians 14:5.

Pray for interpretation — 1 Corinthians 14:13, 27.

If there is no interpreter, then keep silent, but pray in tongues under your breath if you so desire — 1 Corinthians 14:28.

Tongues and interpretation are to be of a limited number — 1 Corinthians 14:23, 27.

Remember, praying in tongues is a commandment of the Lord and is not to be forbidden — 1 Corinthians 14:37, 39.

Also remember that the Lord's church is even where only two or three are gathered together in His name. Thus, a prayer group is His church — Matthew 18:20.

11

What Should We Do with the Power Given to Us by the Baptism in the Holy Spirit?

Jesus' effective ministry commenced after this baptism. We ought to follow His example — Matthew 3:13–17; Mark 1:9–11; Luke 3:21–22; John 1:29–34.

The effective ministry of the apostles and other disciples, after the Resurrection, commenced after this baptism — Acts 2:14–41.

Paul's ministry also began after this baptism — Acts 9:17–18.

Get to know your Bible, read it, study it — John 6:63; 14:26; 15:26; 16:13–15.

Edify, strengthen, and build up yourself in spiritual growth, so as to be able to carry out the other commands of the Lord in His church — 1 Corinthians 14:4; Ephesians 3:16; Jude 20.

Edify, strengthen, and build up the church; be eager to excel in the manifestations of the Spirit in order to edify the church — 1 Corinthians 14:4–5, 12, 19, 26, 31; Acts 20:28.

Be witnesses for Jesus Christ and the Gospel — Matthew 28:19–20; 12:28; Mark 16:15–20; Ephesians 6:18–20; 1 Thessalonians 4:4; Luke 24:47–49; John 20:21; Acts 1:8, 20:28.

Your body is now the temple of the Holy Spirit, *"therefore glorify God in your body and in your spirit, which are God's"* — 1 Corinthians 6:19–20; 3:16–17.

Walk in the Spirit — Galatians 5:25–26.

Do not grieve the Holy Spirit — Ephesians 4:30.

12

What is the Fruit of the Holy Spirit?

The love of God in your heart — Romans 5:5.

Love for others — 1 Corinthians 13:4–8, 13.

The components of love: joy, peace, longsuffering, gentleness, goodness, faith, meekness, righteousness, temperance, truth, power, and a sound mind — Galatians 5:22–23; Romans 14:17; Ephesians 5:9; 2 Timothy 1:7; John 7:38–39.

Remember, you are no holier after receiving the baptism than you were before.

But you now potentially have the power of Jesus within you to overcome evil. The Lord God lets it be your choice, your free will, as to how you use this wonderful gift of God, or whether you bury this talent in the earth — Matthew 25:14–30.

13

How to Receive the Baptism in the Holy Spirit

Become converted, and then become as a little child — Matthew 18:3; Mark 10:15.

Conversion must come first — Ezekiel 36:26–27; John 3:3, 5; Acts 2:38–39; 8:14–17.

Obey the Great Commandment — Matthew 22:35–38; Luke 10:27.

Obey God — Acts 5:32.

Have faith — Acts 2:1–4; 4:31; 10:44.

Let your faith stand in the power of God, not in the wisdom of men — 1 Corinthians 2:4–8.

Determine to know only Christ crucified — 1 Corinthians 2:2.

Relax and surrender every bit of yourself to God, especially your mind and your pride in intellect and worldly wisdom, for they mean nothing to God and are foolishness to Him — 1 Corinthians 1:17–19; Isaiah 29:13–14; 1 Corinthians 3:18–19; James 4:6–7, 10.

Your education can be a hindrance. D.D.'s and Ph.D.'s have a rough time receiving the Spirit until they set aside their human wisdom — 1 Corinthians 1:20–28; 3:18–19.

The laying on of hands sometimes helps but is not always necessary — Acts 8:17; 10:44; 19:6; 2 Timothy 1:6.

Ask the Father, and He will give you the baptism in the Holy Spirit — Luke 11:11–13.

Now, speak forth or sing with sounds that are entirely strange to you. Make the sounds (which are words in a language you do not know) by moving your tongue and lips. The sounds that come forth are a language of the Holy Spirit, praising and magnifying God in a perfect prayer — Acts 2:4, 8–11; 10:46.

Paul said that he desired to both pray and sing with the Spirit — 1 Corinthians 14:15.

The sounds may come haltingly, or seem to stumble, at first, but this is entirely due to your own hesitancy and not that of the Spirit. He wants to praise God through your lips! So keep at it. Do not fail to pray with the Spirit several times, or more, each day. The wonder and glory of it will grow on you, and you will never be at a loss as to how to pray or what to pray about — Romans 8:26–27.

14

What May Happen after Receiving the Baptism in the Holy Spirit?

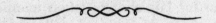

You may be tempted by Satan, as Jesus was, to doubt that you have received the baptism — Matthew 4:1; Mark 1:12–13; Luke 4:1–2.

The Devil may cause you to think, "This is me doing the tongues; this is all foolishness." Here is the first test of your faith, for Satan is really interested in you now. Just continue praying in the Spirit, no matter how foolish it may sound, and Jesus will win out for you. For you now have His Spirit in you, the power of the Holy Spirit, to help you overcome Satan. Remember, *"It is written"* — Matthew 4:3–11; Luke 4:3–12.

You may be delivered up before persecutors — Matthew 10:16–22; Mark 13:11; Luke 12:11–12; 21:12–15; 2 Timothy 3:12; 1 Peter 4:12–14.

You may be teaching and preaching — Matthew 28:19–20; Mark 16:15, Luke 24:47; Ephesians 6:18–20.

You may be here for the coming of Christ for His church, when manifestations of the Holy Spirit will cease, for they will no longer be needed in His presence — 1 Corinthians 13:8–10.

You may be tempted to use tongues only occasionally in private prayer. Don't stunt your spiritual growth; rather, always pray in the Spirit — Ephesians 6:18–20; 1 Corinthians 14:18; 1 Timothy 4:14.

15

The Unforgivable Sin: Blasphemy against the Holy Spirit

All sins and blasphemies will be forgiven except that against the Holy Spirit — Matthew 12:31–32; Mark 3:28–29; Luke 12:10; Hebrews 6:4–6.

16

Reasons Used to Reject the Baptism in the Holy Spirit

Rejection of the Holy Spirit took place even before Christ, when the Holy

Spirit was with the prophets — Acts 7:51.

Full acceptance of God, Jesus, and the Holy Spirit requires the faith of a child — Matthew 18:3; Mark 10:15.

Jesus was rejected by those in high places, by most of the religious leaders, by the successful businesspeople, by the intellectuals, and even by some of His disciples who "fell away" from Him. So it is today with the baptism in the Holy Spirit — John 6:66; 12:42–43; Acts 7:51; 1 Corinthians 1:26.

Prior to their baptism in the Holy Spirit, hundreds of clergymen and laypeople of the so-called denominational churches believed in one or more of the objections set forth below. But when they followed Jesus' command to search the Scriptures, their objections were melted away in the purifying fires of God's holy Word — John 5:39; 1 Corinthians 2:4–8.

Some principal objections to the baptism are as follows.

Objection #1
The baptism in the Holy Spirit
was only for the early church.

a. This is an attempt to limit God. There are no man-made time limitations in God's kingdom.

"But, beloved, do not forget this one thing, that with the Lord one day is as a thousand years, and a thousand years as one day" — 2 Peter 3:8. See also Acts 2:16–21; Hebrews 1:1–2; 1 Peter 1:20.

b. The Lord can do anything and everything today that He has ever done—as He will, where He will, when He will, and with whom He will.

"Jesus Christ is the same yesterday, today, and forever" — Hebrews 13:8.

c. God does not have His children waste His time by having them read something in His Word that is of no use to them today — John 14:12.

d. With the baptism now being received by both the clergy and laity of most Christian churches, this is a further fulfillment of the prophecy of Joel that began at Pentecost.

"And it shall come to pass afterward that I will pour out My Spirit on all flesh" — Joel 2:28.

"For the promise is to you and to your children, and to all who are afar off, as many as the Lord our God will call" — Acts 2:39.

"That the Gentiles should be fellow heirs, of the same body, and partakers of His promise in Christ through the gospel" — Ephesians 3:6.

Objection #2
Tongues are of the Devil.

a. This statement is not supported either by the Scriptures or by experience. If the statement were true, the Devil, with his hatred of Jesus, would use tongues to have us curse our Lord. The Scriptures tell us not only that this is impossible, but also that Satan and his minions cannot understand tongues. Only the Holy Spirit has the gift of the true interpretation — 1 Corinthians 2:7–8; 12:3; 14:2.

b. Experience proves that this is a lie of Satan, because the Devil hates tongues. Often Satan attacks people who are calling upon the name of Jesus and His precious shed blood, who are giving the word of their testimony, and who are praying in tongues. Many times these people can actually feel Satan flee, and they feel the precious love of Christ take over while they are praying in tongues — Revelation 12:11; 1 Corinthians 14:18.

c. Experience shows that people who pray often in tongues in their private devotions achieve the following results:

- They love God more and more as the Father, as the Son, and as the Holy Spirit.
- They understand how a person can die joyfully.
- They love their neighbor, particularly those whom they formerly considered "unlovable."

39

- They love the Bible above all other literature.
- They love to witness and talk about Jesus.
- They have a holy joy in the midst of pain and tribulation.

d. This is what the baptism in the Holy Spirit is accomplishing, through the gift of speaking in unknown tongues, in people of the old-line denominational churches who receive this baptism from God. How can tongues be of the Devil?

Objection #3
Tongues are the least of the gifts.

a. There is no direct scriptural reference to this effect, but note what Paul said about the gift of speaking in tongues.

"I thank my God I speak with tongues more than you all" — 1 Corinthians 14:18.

"I wish you all spoke with tongues" — 1 Corinthians 14:5.

"Do not forbid to speak with tongues"
— 1 Corinthians 14:39.

b. This attack may be answered
with Jesus' own statements about "the
least."

*"If you then are not able to do the
least, why are you anxious for the rest?"*
— Luke 12:26. See also Matthew 5:19;
13:31–32; 25:40; Luke 9:48; 16:10.

Objection #4
It is emotionalism.

a. What did God give us emotions for?
The Great Commandment is to love God
with everything we have. How can you
love, and leave out emotion? The soul or
heart, one or the other, is the seat of the
emotions, and we are commanded to love
God with all our hearts and souls as well
as our minds — Matthew 22:37.

b. What is music in our churches
supposed to accomplish if it does not
touch the emotions? If you see or hear
about the antics of someone who has

received the baptism, remember that if the love of God is in the heart, the antics are never undignified in His eyes, although they may be in the eyes of man — Hebrews 5:7–9; Acts 2:12–16.

"But God has chosen the foolish things of the world to put to shame the wise" — 1 Corinthians 1:27.

"Jesus wept" — John 11:35.

c. Lukewarmness is despised by Jesus — Revelation 3:15–16.

Objection #5
Tongues are not necessary, so we should leave them out of the Christian experience.

a. This is attempting to tell Jesus Christ how His Holy Spirit is to behave. This is a way of forbidding to speak in tongues, which goes against the commandment of the Lord — 1 Corinthians 14:37–39.

b. This is also a failure to fully surrender everything to God, for the tongue is the member of the body that can do

the most good and the most harm —
James 3:2–10.

Objection #6
**These people are selfish; they think they
have something that others do not have.**

a. Of course they have, and so do
those who have salvation! The Scriptures
tell us that those who have received
Christ are a special people — Titus 2:14;
1 Peter 2:9.

b. Almost everyone has something
more in some respect than others—more
education, more money, better health,
better looks, a better marriage, more
freedom, or more love for God. But those
with the full infilling of the Holy Spirit
are far from selfish, for they all want
everyone else to have it, too, and will
lovingly spend all kinds of time and ef-
fort to help others to receive it.

*"As each one has received a gift, min-
ister it to one another, as good stewards
of the manifold grace of God"* — 1 Peter
4:10.

Objection #7
Sure, tongues are scriptural, but I don't need them for assurance that I have the baptism.

a. The one manifestation that satisfied the apostles and the other disciples that a person had received the baptism was speaking in an unknown tongue — Acts 11:1–4, 15, 17–18.

b. There are many people, especially clergy, who have felt this way until they have come in close contact with people who have fully received. Then, when the former finally received the fullness of the baptism, they felt that they had not had it before—that the Spirit had been with them but not in them — John 14:17.

c. Paul felt that praying in an unknown tongue went far beyond just an assurance of having received the baptism.
"I wish you all spoke with tongues" — 1 Corinthians 14:5.

"I thank my God I speak with tongues more than you all" — 1 Corinthians 14:18.

Objection #8
Why don't the Scriptures record that Jesus spoke in an unknown tongue?

a. How could He? What tongues were unknown to Jesus? He knew all languages. He was given *"dominion and glory and a kingdom, that all... languages should serve Him"* — Daniel 7:14. And John the Baptist said, *"God does not give the Spirit by measure"* — John 3:34.

b. Jesus was never limited and never will be — Hebrews 13:8.

People who receive the baptism in the Holy Spirit must be hungry enough for Jesus to want to receive everything that He has for them. They must do so with such faith that they will gladly accept whatever comes in any way that He chooses to give it.

"Nevertheless not My will, but Yours, be done" — Luke 22:42.

17

Is It True? Is It Real? Does It Work?

The documented and oral testimonies of thousands of clergymen and laypeople from practically every Christian church that has received this wonderful blessing bear witness that the answer is a glorious "Yes!" They will tell you that the Bible has become truly alive to them — John 14:26.

The Christ who is now in these believers speaks words of wisdom and of knowledge, heals the sick, works miracles, strengthens faith, discerns good and evil spirits, prays in and interprets tongues, and prophesies —1 Corinthians 12:7–10.

It is indeed the age of the Holy Spirit — Joel 2:28–29.

Keep one last thing in mind: *"But as it is written: 'Eye has not seen, nor ear heard, nor have entered into the heart of man the things which God has prepared for those who love Him.' But God has revealed them to us through His Spirit. For the Spirit searches all things, yes, the deep things of God"* — 1 Corinthians 2:9–10.